1,000,000 Books
are available to read at

www.ForgottenBooks.com

Read online
Download PDF
Purchase in print

ISBN 978-0-656-60098-4
PIBN 11289110

This book is a reproduction of an important historical work. Forgotten Books uses state-of-the-art technology to digitally reconstruct the work, preserving the original format whilst repairing imperfections present in the aged copy. In rare cases, an imperfection in the original, such as a blemish or missing page, may be replicated in our edition. We do, however, repair the vast majority of imperfections successfully; any imperfections that remain are intentionally left to preserve the state of such historical works.

Forgotten Books is a registered trademark of FB &c Ltd.
Copyright © 2018 FB &c Ltd.
FB &c Ltd, Dalton House, 60 Windsor Avenue, London, SW19 2RR.
Company number 08720141. Registered in England and Wales.

For support please visit www.forgottenbooks.com

1 MONTH OF FREE READING

at
www.ForgottenBooks.com

By purchasing this book you are eligible for one month membership to ForgottenBooks.com, giving you unlimited access to our entire collection of over 1,000,000 titles via our web site and mobile apps.

To claim your free month visit:
www.forgottenbooks.com/free1289110

* Offer is valid for 45 days from date of purchase. Terms and conditions apply.

English
Français
Deutsche
Italiano
Español
Português

www.forgottenbooks.com

Mythology Photography **Fiction** Fishing Christianity **Art** Cooking Essays **Buddhism** Freemasonry Medicine **Biology** Music **Ancient Egypt** Evolution Carpentry Physics Dance Geology **Mathematics** Fitness Shakespeare **Folklore** Yoga Marketing **Confidence** Immortality Biographies Poetry **Psychology** Witchcraft Electronics Chemistry History **Law** Accounting **Philosophy** Anthropology Alchemy Drama Quantum Mechanics Atheism Sexual Health **Ancient History Entrepreneurship** Languages Sport Paleontology Needlework Islam **Metaphysics** Investment Archaeology Parenting Statistics Criminology **Motivational**

Drusilla Poole Col., ANC, received her B.A. degree in social work from Scarritt College in 1942; M.N. from Yale University in 1947; Ph.D. from The University of Texas in 1969. While a student at Yale she also attended the language school, and upon graduation was asked to serve as Instructor and Director of Nursing, Hiang-Ya Hospital, Changsha, Hunan, China. After returning to the U.S.A. and working as a civilian, she entered the Army Nurse Corps.

While on active duty Col. Poole has distinguished herself through a variety of clinical and administrative assignments; Director Department of Nursing Science, MFSS, and Director, WRAIN. She has also been active in civic and professional organizations. In recognition of her achievements Col. Poole was honored as the "Outstanding Army Nurse Corps Officer of 1973."

On the occasion of your planned retirement, we salute you, Col. Poole, and extend to you our best wishes.

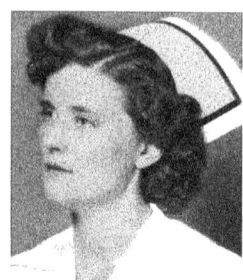

Yale University
1947

Hsiang-Ya Hospital
China, 1948–50

Graduating Class
Hsiang-Ya Hospital

"You give but little when you give of your possessions. It is when you give of yourself that you truly give."

DAR Award — 1973

"The teacher who walks in the shadow of the temple among his followers, gives not of his wisdom but rather of his faith and his lovingness.

From THE PROPHET
Copyright 1923, Renewal copyright 1951 by Administrators C.T.A. of Kahlil Gibran Estate, and Mary G. Gibran. Reprinted by permission of A. Knopf, Inc.

TABLE OF CONTENTS

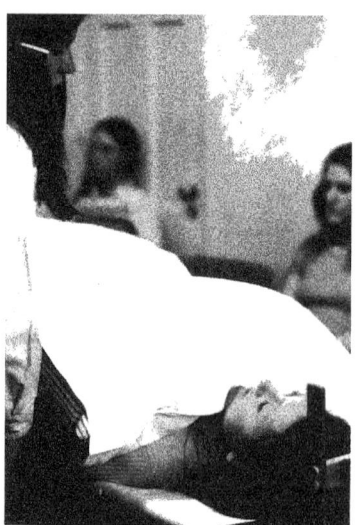

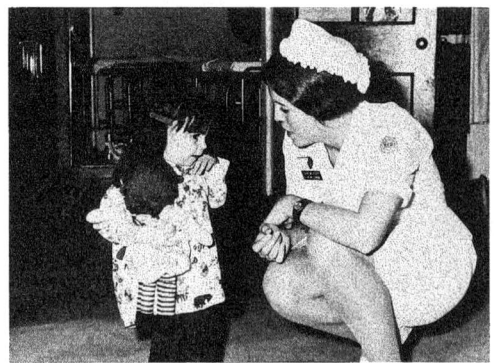

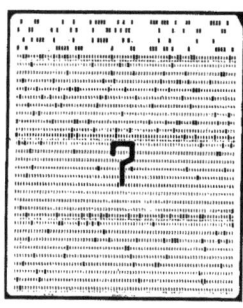
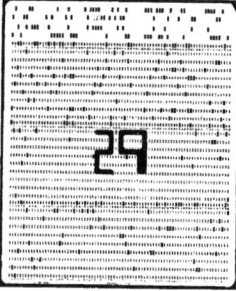
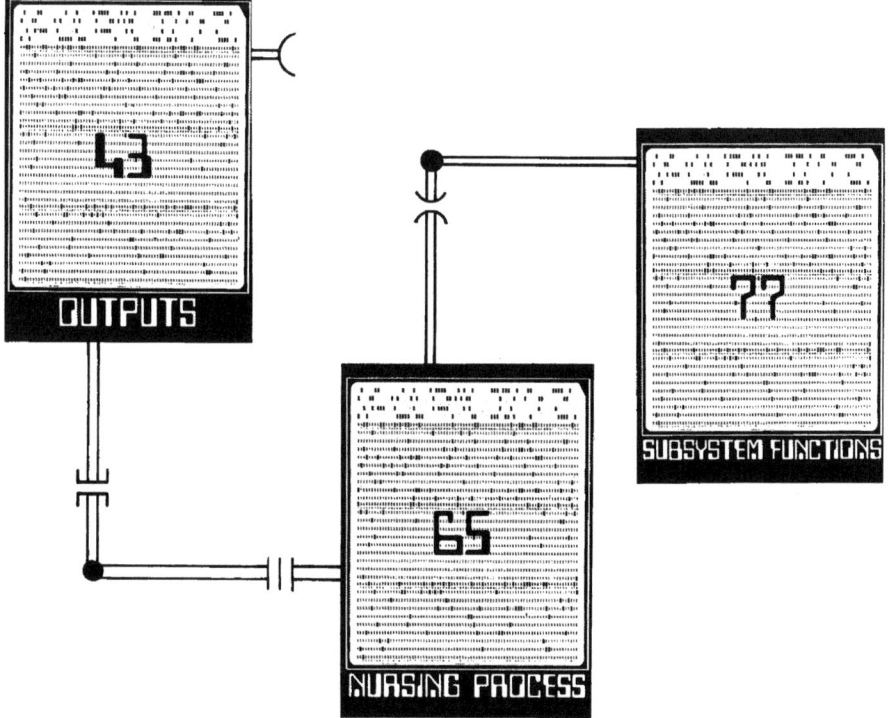

In the Fall of 1972, the University of Maryland School of Nursing implemented a new curriculum designed to educate nursing students using a holistic approach to the study of man. Inherent in this approach was the integration of curriculum content focusing on the biological, psychological, sociological needs of man as the basis for nursing education. The development of a conceptual framework was used to facilitate the study of man, his needs, and the nurses' role in providing care.

The yearbook staff of 1973–74, feels that it is appropriate to utilize this conceptual framework in portraying student life at WRAIN, especially since the class of 1974 is the first to complete this new program.

The environment provided for living and learning is Delano Hall. INPUTS into the student system are provided by the administration, faculty, and staff. OUTPUTS of the student system are graduates prepared to practice as generalists in nursing. The WRAIN students are described as THROUGHPUT of the system experiencing negentrophy, i.e., progressing from less to more complex states of organization. In order for the student system to achieve and/or maintain dynamic equilibrium, they must have SUB-SYSTEM functioning that provides some satisfaction. The activities are depicted as the goal achievement of the sub-systems. The NURSING PROCESS, the clinical section, depicts the nurses' role in providing care.

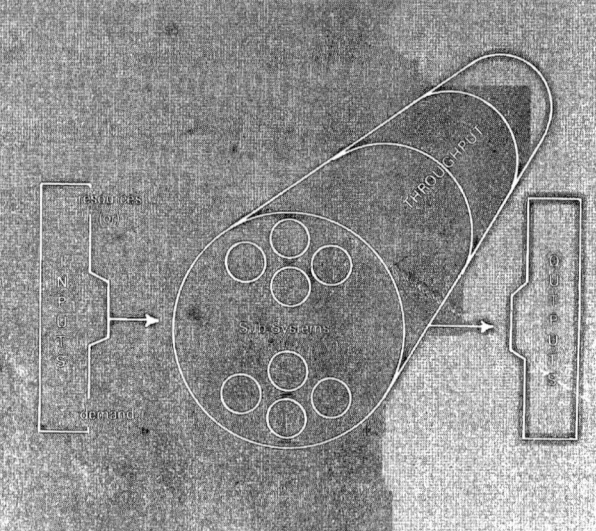

University of Maryland
School of Nursing
Baltimore Campus

Dr. Wilson H. Elkins
President, University of Maryland

Dr. Albin O. Kuhn
Chancellor, University of Maryland,
Baltimore Campus

Dr. Marion I. Murphy
Dean, School of Nursing

Administrations: Baltimore

Dr. Daryl Stewart

Mrs. Barbara Spivack

Dr. Elizabeth Hughes
Director, Senior Curriculum

Miss Elise Michael
Director, Junior Curriculum

WRAIN

COL Drusilla Poole ANC
Director

LTC Marian C. Barbieri ANC
Deputy Director

LTC Norma Small
Senior Cluster Coordinator

LTC Hannah Moynahan
Junior Cluster Coordinator

People

ADJUTANT AND STAFF

MAJ Clara Adams
Educational Coordinator

MAJ John Skelton
Adjutant

PFC Sandy Duffet

1SG Fannie Gray

who help

CPT Ervin Norgren

Sgt Enid Lapage

Mr. Antonio Valerio

SP5 Joseph Ogo

S
U
P
P
L
Y

AUDIO VISUAL

Mr. Billy L.

Mr. J. W. Jackson

Mr. John T. Williams

Audio Visual Lab

SECRETARIES

Mrs. Mazzone

Mrs. Jordan

Mrs. McGovern

Miss Gist

Mrs. Griffin

Miss Robinson, Mrs. Brown, Mrs. Estill

RECEPTIONISTS

Mrs. Roberta Rankin

Mrs. Pansy Clark

Mrs. Mary Railey

RESIDENT COUNSELORS

Mrs. Mary Meighen

Mrs. Florence Ames

Mrs. Virginia Guiteras

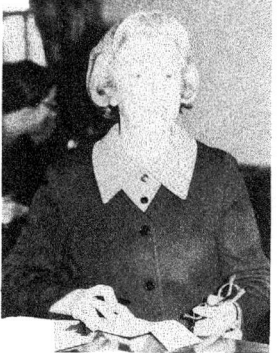
Mrs. Dorothy Hastings

Miss Gwendolyn Brown

Faculty — Resource . . .

COMMUNITY HEALTH NURSING

MAJ Ann N. Ashjian

CPT Caroline Brodkey

Dr. Betty Ruano
Department Chairman

LTC Ellen M. Berg

Mrs. Ellen Doctor

LTC Joyce J. Nurse
Assistant to Chairman

Or Demand?

MAJ Merlan O. Ellis

MAJ Anna K. Frederico

MAJ Eileen L. Fox

CPT Glenn B. Knepper

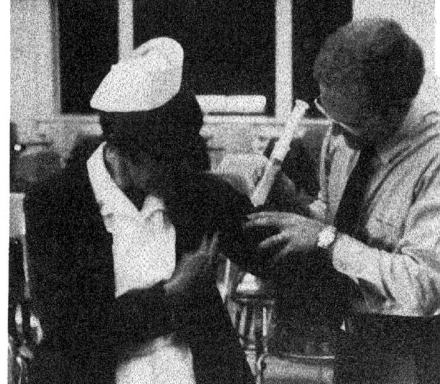

MATERNAL AND CHILD HEALTH NURSING

Dr. Mary Neal
Department Chairman

CPT Elizabeth M. McGowan
Assistant to Chairman

MAJ Betty Brice

Not Pictured —
CPT Elizabeth A. Martin

CPT Rosamond P. Shepard

LTC Eleanor J. Streett

Mrs. Donna Wilsker

LTC Hannah S. Moynahan
Assistant to Chairman

LTC Sarah A. Balkema

MAJ Marsha H. Cohen

MAJ Jean M. Johnson

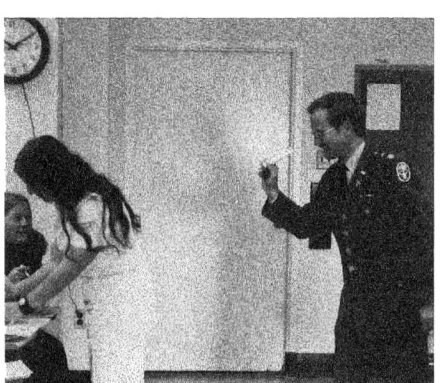
Ready . . . Aim . . . Fire!

CPT Janet S. Rexrode

CPT Margaret Wilson

Not Pictured —
MAJ Eugenia A. Vineys

MEDICAL SURGICAL NURSING

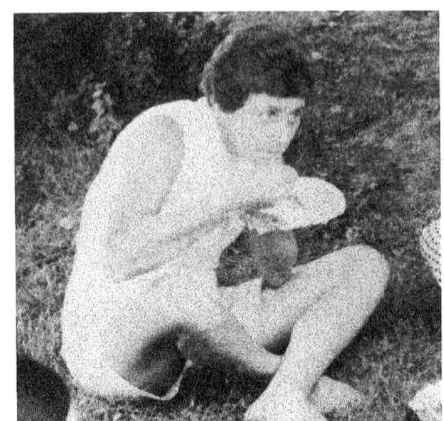

"... and no more meals. You're getting enough between meals."

Dr. Ann Madison
Department Chairman

LTC Francis A. Hiers
Assistant to Chairman

CPT Vonna J. Carroll   MAJ Laura J. Coggin

Not pictured:
MAJ Donna H. Ewing

 MAJ Kathleen Devin
 CPT Barbara L. Lust
 CPT Linda L. Pape
 CPT Faith E. Sterling

 MAJ Richard H. Evert
 LTC Betty J. Lynch
 CPT Elizabeth Ryan
 MAJ Lila C. Stevens

 MAJ Charlotte Jerney
 CPT Joseph P. Maloney
 LTC Norma R. Small
 MAJ Marilyn J. Sylvester

PSYCHIATRIC NURSING

CPT Charles E. Douglas
Assistant to Chairman

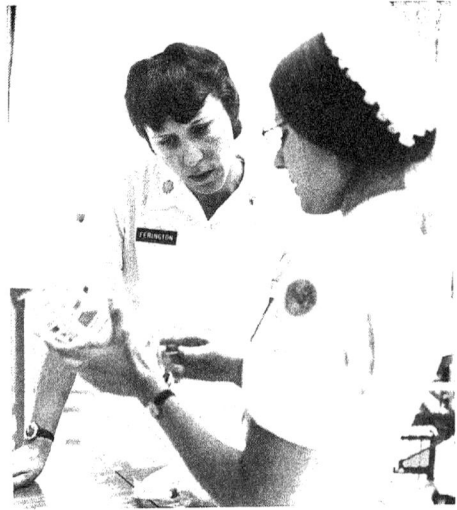

 MAJ Betty J. Antilla

 CPT Mary A. Bailey

 MAJ Corrine Burnett

 MAJ Felicitus E. Ferington

 Mrs. Myra Fisher

 LTC John H. Karwoski

 MAJ Joyce G. Johnson

 CPT Paul C. Learmann

 MAJ Lawrence Washington

PATHOPHYSIOLOGY

PHARMACOLOGY

MAJ James Vick
CPT Bertram A. Nicholas
Not Pictured —
 CPT Jurgen VonBredow

NUTRITION

LTC Eleanor J. Strayer
1LT Jesse Majkowski

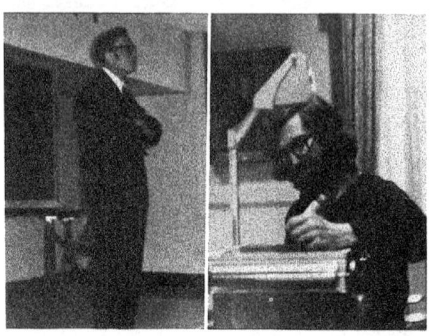

Dr. Matthew R. Tayback —
Biostatistics
Dr. Robert Ashmore —
Human Development
Not Pictured —
Dr. Cletus R. Brady — Social Problems
Mrs. Miriam Rothchild — Nursing Research

"Human" Side of a Uniform . . .?

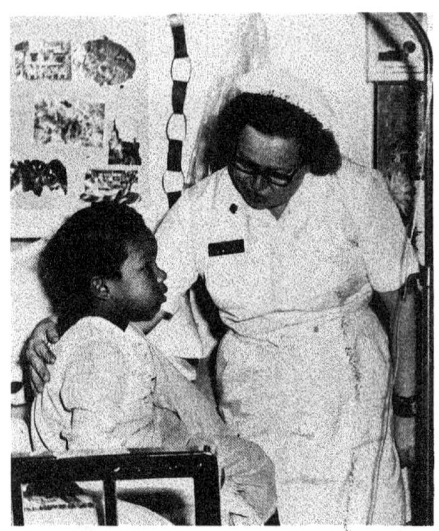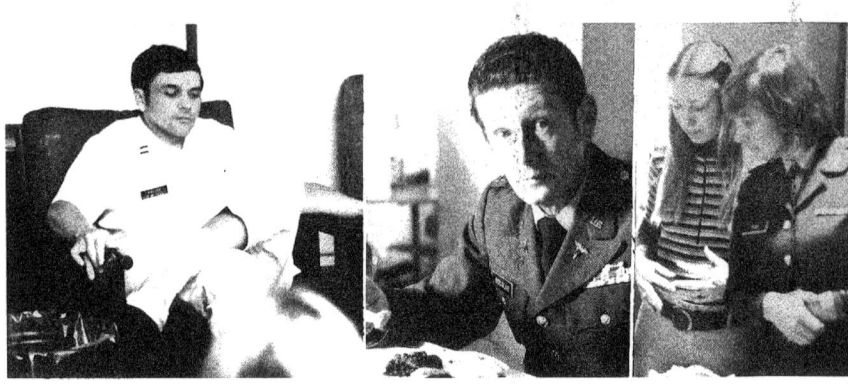

. . . And with a little help from our friends! . . .

JUNIOR CLASS

MAJ Betty Brice — Advisor; Jane Roeger — Vice President; Carolyn Sanger — SGO Social Chmn.; Mary Kay Kramer — Treasurer; Jim Parham — President; Gail Velguth — Social Chmn.; Mary Ann Averell — SGO Secretary; Karen Lorbert — Secretary; Jacki Mettey — Unit Fund Representative

Mardi Bartholdt   Susan Beatty
Robin Bechtel   Deborah Bechtold
Rita Behlen   Debra Bernard

Joanne Ade   Jonnie Allen   Estelita Almachar
Mary Anderson   Vicki Anderson   Maryanne Averell
Kathleen Baehr Deborah Bannister Cecilia Bartel

Jenny Bernard   Kathryn Bird   Steve Booker

Karen Boyle   Shirley Bratrud   Marsha Brock

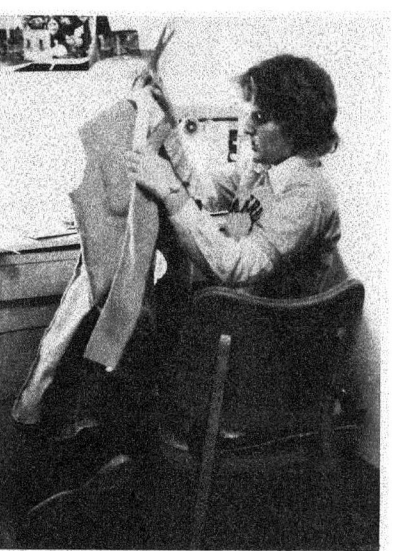

Deborah Brown   Diane Brown   Elizabeth Brown   Rebecca Burchfield   Kathryn Burg

Kathryn Burns   Paula Butler

Kerry Byers Jan Carlson Linda Chancey Cynthia Cvelbar June Dail

Jean Dailey Margaret Dapra Linda Dawson

Leslie Dempsey Lynette Dickey Gretchen Dickrell

Barbara Disch Janet Dover Deborah Doyle

Noreen Driscoll Barbara Eller Mary J. Evans

Rosalie Ewing Gayle Fletcher Kathleen France Karen Fred Carolyn Fritz

Denice Gambill Linda George Jean Gilbert

Regina Girlando

Margaret Goeckler

Carolyn Goucher

Eleanor Greenwood

Arlene Gross

Debra Haeder

Kathleen Hapke

Cynthia Hawley

Mary Jo Heifers

Eileen Hill

Rhonda Hobbs

Margaret Hoisington

Renita Holland

Jane Horvat

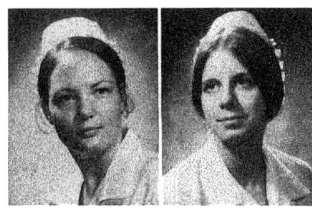

Patricia Howland   Carol Humke

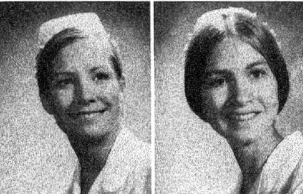

Jan Iken   Paula Jackan

Bethanie Jasper   Nancy Jerde   Barbara Johnson   Charlotte Johnson   Pamela Key

Patricia Kinder   Pamela Kishaba   Linda Klein   Keri Klotzbuecher

Carolyn Kraft Mary Kramer Susan Kryst Deborah Landis

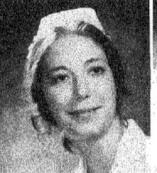   

Julie Lane Kaureen Langlie Brenda Lansberry Gayle Leary

Brenda Leiding Anne Leisering Cecily Light Alyce Lipps Karen Lorbert

Marian Machman Patricia McLean Linda McMorris Carol McNeil

Theresa Markstrum Jacki Mettey

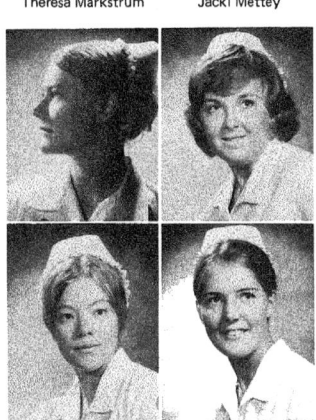

Robin Miles Patricia Miller

Martha Montie   Bonnie Moreland   Charlotte Murison   Mary Murphy

Ann Norton   Judy O'Leary

| Patricia O'Neill | Linda Opdycke | James Parham | Mary Pearson |
| Jane Peek | Katherine Penn | Mark Petersen | Helen Peterson |

| Janet Petroske | Marilyn Phillips | Sharon Ponce | Karen Reichel | Kathleen Rendos |

Teresa Rincon   Rosemarie Ritchie

Teresa Robinson Jane Roeger
Rebecca Rubio Carolyn Sanger
Jeri Secord Audrey Shadd
Jeanne Stoepker

Priscilla Suess Phyllis Snyder Roberta Troxell
Michael Tucker Denise Vandergriff Debbie VanTine

Gail Velguth   Debra Vilendrer   Dolores Vissers   Sandra Weiss   Jane Westphal

Kathryn Whittenberg   Lanell Woods

Teresa Wright   Teresa Young

Not Pictured

Kris Bushouse
Helen Dorsey
Ellen Dougherty
Lynne Kehrli
Linda Key
Alexis Keyson
Katherine Kingsford
Brenda Lilly
Mary Martin
Chris Miller
Marni Mundt

Gail Nelson
Liisa Nenonen
Pat O'Connor
Jeanne Picariello
Jean Simmons
Janie Trettin
Juliana Warner
Lola Whaley
Chris Whitmire
Janet Zdybek

T
H
E

C
L
A
S
S

O
F

1
9
7
4

SENIOR CLASS OFFICERS

L. to R. Maureen Shrewsbury, Secretary; Barbara Zurawski, Vice-President; Beth Conover, Social Co-Chairman; Pat Root, Senior Senator; Sarah Fearn, President; Sandi Bolt, Social Co-Chairman; and Carol Sassaman, Treasurer.

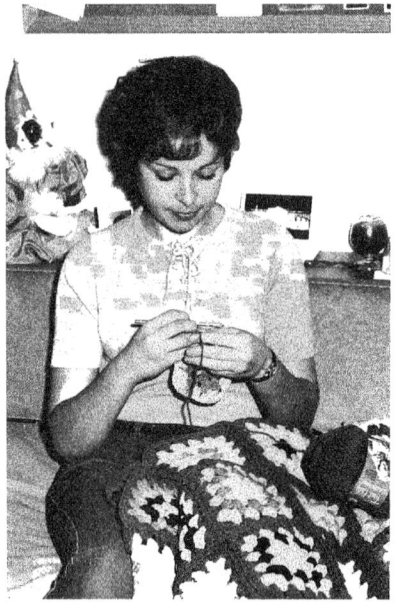

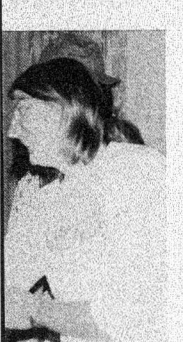

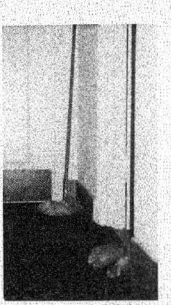

Being a Senior is FUN, EXHAUSTING, AND SCARRY!
It means the END of: term papers, handouts, exams and being a WRAIN student.
Symbolic of the END are: Cap Stringing, Convocation, Commencement, and Commissioning.
It means the BEGINNING of: new places, new people, travel, and an EXCITING FUTURE.

Jo-Bette Akers
Kythrine Allen

Sharon Andrews
Mary Arata

Kathleen Baish
Barbara Bala
Claire Baldwin

 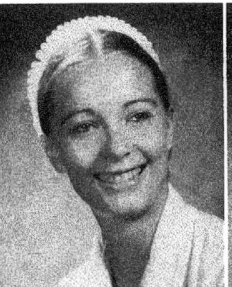  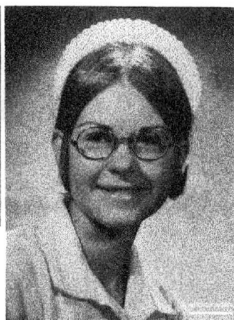

Bobby Berg   Eileen Berlin

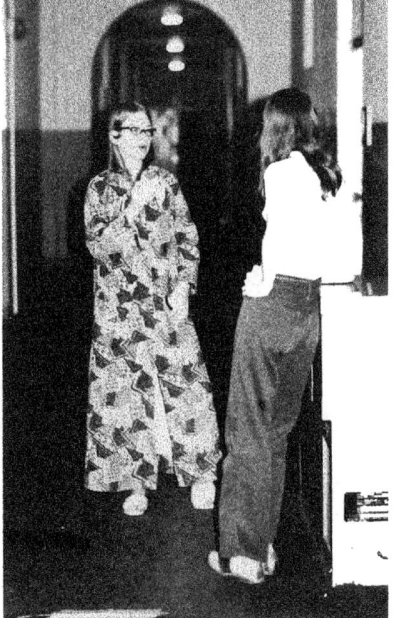

Joyce Ball
Rose Barnett
Janice Benonis

Marlene Berlin
Norma Beyer
Jane Blaase

Bernadette Caporale
Karoline Carlson

Candace Carrico
Patricia Cartwright

Rozanne Blake
Sandra Bolt
Patricia Borup

Phyllis Brosius
Patsy Browning
Nina Bryson

Lorna Chatmon
Leslie Clark
Diana Combs

Elizabeth Conover
Karen Conte
Christine Dallenbach

Mary Davis

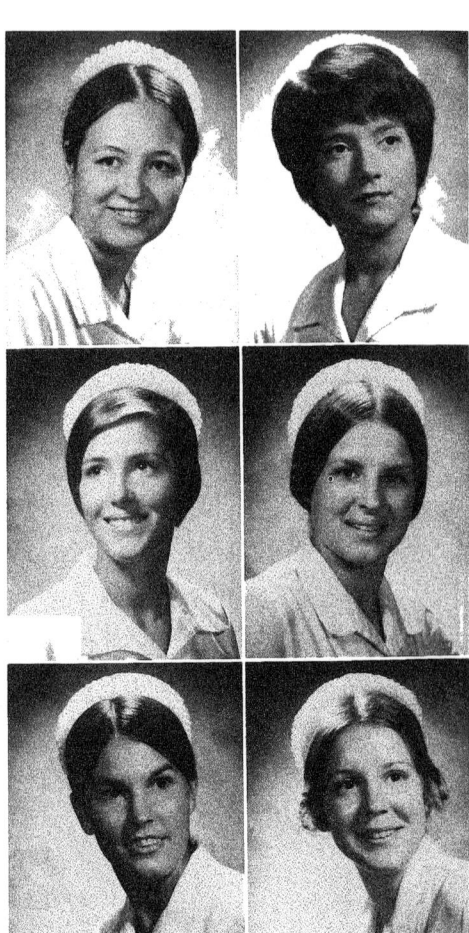

Barbara De Long
Kathleen Deska
Sarah Fearn

Barbara Fede
Carolyn Fint
Patricia Flanagan

Dinah Halopka
Barbara Hammond

Madelyn Foley
Catherine Fons
Susan Forney

Richard Fortune
Marie Franklin
Rebecca Gilliam

Sandra Goodale
Karen Green
Madonna Griffey

  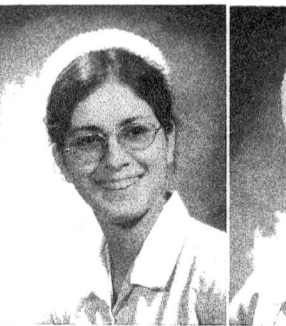 

Dorothy Jaeger
Janet Jefferson

Deborah Johnson
Ethelyn Johnson

Gaynelle Hancock
Cheryl Heath
Vicky Hessling

Cathy Hulbert
David Hundley
Margaret Ianovale

Teresa Kelly
Pamela Klein

Susan Kotarski
Janet Lawing

Wilma Johnson
Jo Ellen Johnston
Deborah Jones

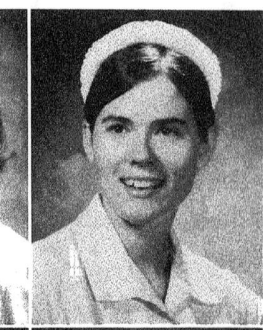

Leslie Lloyd

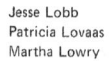

Jesse Lobb
Patricia Lovaas
Martha Lowry

Maureen Malone
Valerie Marchant
Theresa Marks

Linda Marx
Gerardine McCarty

Catherine McGuane
Mary Meredith

Barbara Meyer
Carol Morrell
Kim Morrissey

Sarah Mottley
Bonnie Muse
Patricia Mussnug

Margaret Ann Nelson
Patricia Nelson

Alison Nilmag
Ellen O'Connor

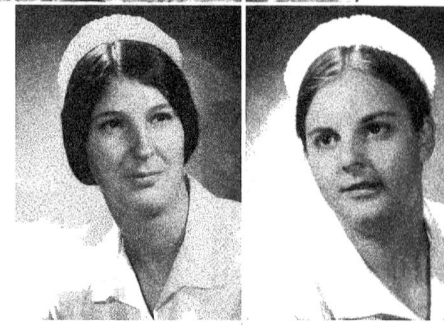

Teresa Penin

Lee Pilkanis

Deborah Rank
Diane Rapalas
Dianne Reali

Catherine Reed
Marylou Robinson
Susan Rogers

Patricia Root
Belle Rowan

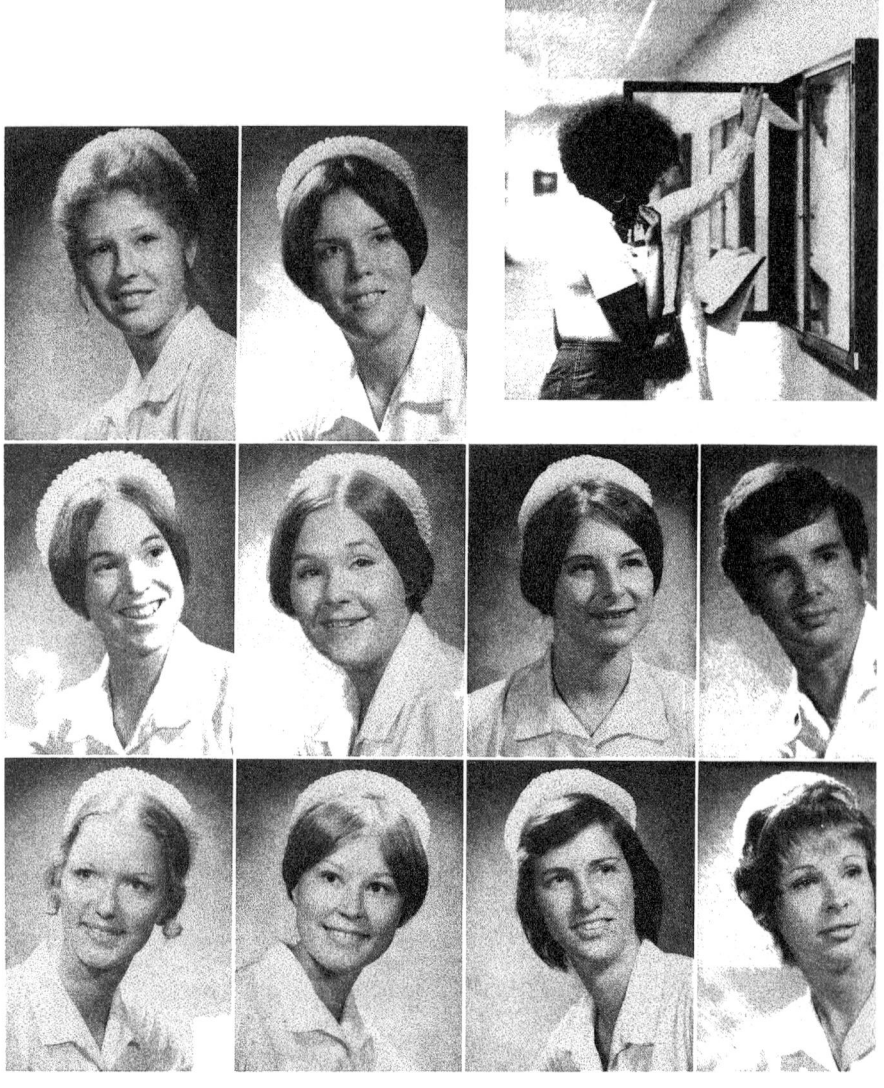

Carol Sassaman
Marcia Scheider
Roslyn Shelton

Maureen Shrewsbury
Ellen Simmerman
Catherine Skidmore

Kathleen D. Smith
Kathleen N. Smith

William Spring
Nancy Steele

Teresa Ann Ulrich
Jeanette Ward

Paula Wink
Roberta Wolfe

Patricia Sweeney
Ernestine Thomas
Janet Traylor

Barbara Zurawski

Susan Wood
Bridget Woodruff

Christy Woxland
Christine Yank

Kay Yeager
Susan Young

Not Pictured

Peggy Allen
Patricia Burke
Pearline Butcher
Patricia Clark
Kathy Connor
Kathryn Forsythe
Milda Frederiksen

Charla Fryer
Cindy Gale
Diane Henderson
Karen Kuehn
Louise Kurdys
Colleen Russell
Patricia Smith

SENIOR DIRECTORY

AKERS, Jo-Bette
c/o Geo. B. Akers
1847 Fifth St.
Manhattan Beach, Calif. 90266

ALLEN, Kythrine B.
c/o Bryants
4410 West Hill Trail
Amarillo, Texas 79106

ALLEN, Peggy A.
c/o M. Max Allen
934 Oakwood Trail
Indianapolis, Indiana 46260

ANDREWS, Sharon E.
c/o R. M. Andrews
3192 Owen Hollow Rd.
Big Flats, N. Y. 14814

ARATA, Mary M.
c/o Dr. J. Herrington
2122 W. 53rd St.
Milwaukee, Wisc.

BAISH, Kathleen M.
c/o COL (Ret.) C. F. Baish
450 Chase Dr.
Corpus Christi, Texas 78412

BALA, Barbara A.
c/o F. Bala
310 Ruth Ave.
Maple Shade, N.J. 08052

BALDWIN, Claire E.
c/o F. S. Baldwin
4 Briggs Road
Cornwall-On-Hudson, N.Y.

BALL, Joyce E.
c/o Mrs. E. Barry
13243 1st Ave. So.
Seattle, Wash. 98168

BARNETT, Rose H.
c/o O. R. Harford
Box 36
Clarksburg, Ind. 47225

BENONIS, Janice W.
c/o C. P. Wilcox
Apt. 105
13015 Twinbrook Pkwy.
Rockville, Md. 20851

BERG, Bobby A.
c/o O. Berg
RR #1
Red Wing, Minn.

BERLIN, Eileen K.
c/o R. Berlin
2 W. 2nd St.
El Paso, Ill. 61738

BERLIN, Marlene J.
c/o R. Berlin
2 W. 2nd St.
El Paso, Ill. 61738

BEYER, Norma H.
c/o Mrs. G. P. Hopkins
3216 Northgate Dr.
Virginia Beach, Va. 23452

BLAASE, Jane A.
c/o R. L. Blaase
460 E. Broadway
Argenta, Ill. 62501

BLAKE, Rozanne M.
c/o P. Kirk
10518 Asterdid
San Antonio, Texas 78217

BOLT, Sandra M.
c/o A. J. Munoz
1924 Pinetree Rd.
Trenton, Mich.

BORUP, Patricia A.
c/o Mrs. J. Borup
677 G St., Sp. 8
Chula Vista, Calif. 92010

BROSIUS, Phyllis M.
c/o R. Brosius
550 Church St.
Millersburg, Pa. 17061

BROWNING, Patsy L.
c/o I. L. Browning
3816 14th Ave. SE
Largo, Fla.

BRYSON, Nina
c/o Dr. M. Bryson
2580 Tierra Grande
Carmel Valley, Calif. 93921

BURKE, Patricia J.
c/o John Burke
P.O. Box 20142
Orlando, Fla.

BUTCHER, Pearline M.
c/o L. P. Butcher
9332 E. Canfield
Detroit, Mich. 48214

CAPORALE, Bernadette
c/o L. Caporale
13007 Forest Glen Rd.
Woodbridge, Va. 22191

CARLSON, Karoline L.
c/o R. N; Carlson
Box 216
Kerkhoven, Minn.

CARRICO, Candace K.
c/o LTC (Ret.) J. Kirsch
9308 Mathis Ave.
Manassas, Va. 22110

CARTWRIGHT, Patricia R.
c/o Cartwrights
710 Grant St.
Canton, Mo.

CHATMON, Lorna R.
c/o Mrs. M. Norman
157-10 Riverside Drive W.
New York, New York

CLARK, Leslie A.
c/o W. Clark
4455 Dale Ave.
La Mesa, Calif. 92041

CLARK, Patricia A.
c/o H. Clark
2132 Quirinal Ct.
Fenton, Mo. 63026

COMBS, Diana J.
c/o Mr. J. Combs
3675 Midland Ave.
White Bear Lake, Minn. 55110

CONNOR, Kathy A.
c/o LCDR E. E. Connor
132 Corsair
NAS LeMoore, Calif.

CONOVER, Elizabeth A.
c/o R. E. Conover
401 Slocum Ave
Neptune, N.J. 07753

CONTE, Karen E.
c/o A. L. Conte
27186 Pompton Dr.
North Olmsted, Ohio 44070

DALLENBACH, Christine A.
c/o L. A. Dallenbach
133 Outcalt St.
Hightstown, N. J. 08520

DAVIS, Mary C.
c/o F. Davis
Rt. 1, Box 12
Wakefield, Va. 23888

De LONG, Barbara K.
c/o Kirks
9 Ruth Dr.
Wilbraham, Mass. 01095

DESKA, Kathleen A.
c/o E. Deska
217 Centennial Rd.
Warminsten, Pa.

FEARN, Sarah L.
c/o Cpt. W. R. Fern
Governor's Island, N.Y., N.Y. 10004

FEDE, Barbara A.
c/o S. A. Fede
Springville Heights Rd.
Box 168 B
Darlington, S. C.

FINT, Carolyn H.
c/o R. W. Hall
11715 W. 30th Pl.
Lakewood, Colo.

FLANAGAN, Patricia H.
c/o W. S. Flanagan
416 Central St.
Saugus, Mass. 01906

FLOYD, Marcia J.
c/o COL M. B. Scheider
4829 Willet Dr.
Annandale, Va.

FOLEY, Madelyn C.
c/o C. Foley
219 7th Ave.
Shell Lake, Wisc.

FONS, Catherine A.
c/o D. E. Fons
3385 S. 119 St.
West Allis, Wisc. 53227

FORNEY, Susan V.
c/o Forney
2616 Laurel
Waterloo, Iowa

FORSYTHE, Kathryn M.
c/o G. L. Forsythe
4920 S. Jonathan La.
New Berlin, Wisc. 53151

FORTUNE, Richard N.
333 West Side Dr.
#201
Gaithersburg, Md. 20760

FRANKLIN, Angela
c/o R. E. Franklin
Box 277
412 Carlyle St.
Payne, Ohio 45880

FREDERIKSEN, Milda A.
c/o G. Frederiksen
8449 W. Vassar Dr.
Lakewood, Colo.

FRYER, Charla K.
c/o A. Fryer
3128 Roosevelt Rd.
Kenosha, Wisc. 53140

GALE, Cindy J.
c/o H. F. Gauthier
P. O. Box 4
Salisbury, Md.

GILLIAM, Rebecca A.
c/o W. F. Gilliam
139 Hanover Ave.
Hampton, Va. 23361

GOODALE, Sandra E.
c/o G. S. Goodale
3013 Melissa Dr.
Friendly, Md. 20022

GREEN, Karen K.
c/o P. J. Green
2806 Highwood
Dallas, Texas

GRIFFEY, Madonna L.
c/o R. D. Griffey
4005 N. Kitley
Indianapolis, Ind. 46226

HALOPKA, Dinah L.
c/o R. Halopka
Rt. 1
Stetsonville, Wis 54480

HAMMOND, Barbara J.
c/o R. Hammond
Fedora, S.D

HANCOCK, Gaynelle L.
c/o W. Hancock
230 Braxton Ave.
Salem, Va.

HEATH, Cheryl J.
c/o LTC C. V. Heath
605 Winfield
San Antonio, Tex 70239

HENDERSON, Diane O.
c/o C. O. Osterlund
930 Belle Vista
Martinez, Ca 94553

HESSLING, Vicky E.
c/o Lester Egdorf
RR 1
Glenwood, Minn. 56334

HULBERT, Cathy B.
c/o Dr. L. Hulbert
1461 Pinewood Ave.
Anaheim, Ca 92805

HUNDLEY, David P.
c/o J. Jupin
13304 Ashlawn Dr.
Louisville, Ky

IANOVALE, Margaret T.
c/o J. J. Ianovale
6497 Morris Park Rd.
Philadelphia, Pa 19151

JAEGER, Dorothy M.
c/o J. J. Jaeger
24 Reddin Rd.
Charleston, S.C. 29405

JEFFERSON, Janet C.
c/o J. D. Jefferson
616 Fairlie Road
Colonial Heights, Va

JOHNSON, Deborah D.
c/o J. Davidson
Rt. #1
Stanton, Neb 68779

JOHNSON, Ethelyn D.
c/o R. Johnson
18401 Littlefield
Detroit, Mich.

JOHNSON, Wilma C.
c/o L. S. Clifford

6691 Miller St.
Arvada, Colo

JOHNSTON, Jo Ellen
c/o W. A. Johnston
1 Ross Dr.
Norman, Oklahoma 73069

JONES, Deborah C.
c/o W. Jones
7420 Brentwood Dr.
Stockton, Calif

KELLY, Teresa E.
c/o F. H. Kelly
1152 W. Copper
Butte, Mont. 59701

KLEIN, Pamela J.
c/o D. E. Klein
7020 Palmetto St.
Cincinnati, Ohio 45227

KOTARSKI, Susan K.
c/o G. W. Kotarski
523 Diagonal St.
George, Utah

KUEHN, Karen A.
c/o C. H. Kuehn
R.R. 2
Marcus, Iowa 51035

KURDYS, Louise E.
c/o E. Kurdys
82 Gatchen St.
Buffalo, N.Y.

LAWING, Janet L.
c/o Col. W. S. Lawing
6212 Deveron Dr.
Charlotte, N.C. 28211

LLOYD, Leslie G.
c/o W. E. Greimann
RR #3
Blue Earth, Minn. 56013

LOBB, Jesse A.
c/o H. J. Lobb
918 W. 32nd Terr.
Kansas City, Mo. 64111

LOVAAS, Patricia K.
c/o D. Lovaas
601 19th Ave. N.
Fargo, N.D.

LOWRY, Martha H.
c/o M. H. Hesselman
110 Northview Terr.
Greensburg, Penn. 15601

MALONE, Maureen M.
c/o E. J. Malone
3392 W. Tanforan
Englewood, Colo. 80110

MARCHANT, Valerie P.
c/o J. E. Marchant
15 Columbia St.
Watertown, Mass. 02172

MARKS, Theresa M.
c/o E. G. Marks
3016 N. 121st St.
Wauvatosa, Wis. 53222

MARX, Linda D.
c/o L. G. Marx
1780 Dichter Ct.
Thornton, Colo. 80229

McCARTY, Geraldine J.
c/o F. J. McCarty
R.R. #1
Sanborn, Iowa 51248

McGUANE, Catherine T.
c/o A. J. Tassone
619 Bayne St.
McKeesport, Pa.

MEREDITH, Mary C.
c/o R. A. Meredith
38988 Larkspur St.
Newark, Calif

MEYER, Barbara C.
c/o J. R. Cartwell
Box 38
Belmont, West Va.

MORRELL, Carol E.
c/o E. J. Morrell
19280 Warrington
Detroit, Mich.

MORRISSEY, Kim O.
c/o I. R. Osman
209 Comly Rd.
Apt. 31-K
Lincoln Park, N.J.

MOTTLEY, Sarah A.
c/o J. D. Mottley
Rt. 1, Box 107
Marshall, Va 22115

MUSE, Bonnie Jo
c/o E. C. Muse
1114 Coach Rd.
Homewood, Ill.

MUSSNUG, Patricia L.
c/o M. S. Mussnug
1999 Elliott Dr.
Clearwater, Fla

NELSON, Margaret Ann
c/o A. G. Nelson
537 Rockne Ave.
Massapequa Pk, N.Y. 11762

NELSON, Patricia D.
c/o G. Nelson
R.R. 1
Cecil, Ohio 45821

NILMAG, Alison N.
c/o S. J. Nakanishi
4608 N. Augusta
Fresno, Ca 93726

O'CONNOR, Ellen M.
c/o W. O. O'Connor
102 Manchester Ct.
Wayne, N.J. 07470

PEPIN, Teresa M.
c/o N. Pepin
420 Sec. Ave. No.
Long Prairie, Mn. 56347

PEREZ, Sandra O.
c/o M. Otto
6038 Green Bay Rd.
Oshkosh, Wisc

PICCIOLI, Janice M.
c/o A. Piccioli
Hennepin St.
Mark, Ill 61340

PILKANIS, Lee C.
c/o F. V. Pilkanis
126 Oak Ridge Terr
Lynnfield, Mass 01940

POPPAS, Candace S.
LTC (Ret) G. Poppas
214 Sherwood Dr.
Dothan, Ala

PUTZ, Barbara A.
c/o C. O. Putz
1784 Coolidge
Saginaw, Mich. 48603

RANK, Deborah J.
c/o R. L. Normanly
Crumb Hill Rd.
East Otto, N.Y.

RAPALAS, Diane K.
c/o A. F. Rapalas
3042 W. Cactus Rd.
Phoenix, Ariz. 85029

REALI, Dianne S.
c/o D. F. Starkey
400 N. Main St.
Attica, Ohio

REED, Catherine O.
c/o D. K. Orr
Rt. /4, Box 333
De Soto, Mo 63020

ROBINSON, Marylou V.
c/o W. J. Robinson
11710 Pawnee Dr. S.W.
Tacoma, Wash

ROGERS, Susan B.
c/o Bronson
P. O. Box 3353
Panama City, Fla. 32401

ROOT, Patricia A.
c/o J. Root
11201 Cresent Valley Dr. NW.
Crig Harbor, Wa 98105

ROWAN, Belle B.
c/o B. Hopkins
3531 Kings Rd.
Steger, Ill.

RUSSELL, Colleen L.
c/o H. A. Russell
102 Chamberlain Dr.
Marieta, Ohio 45750

SASSAMAN, Carol A.
c/o T. D. Sassaman
726 N. LaCrosse St.
Allentown, Penn 18103

SHELTON, Roslyn L.
Maj. (Ret) L. C. Shelton
2035 Brent Dr.
Shreveport, La

SHREWSBURY, Maureen A.
c/o J. B. Shrewsbury
636 Craig Woods Dr.
St. Louis, Mo.

SIMMERMAN, Ellen A.
c/o J. S. Simmerman
2917 Aurie Ct.
Decatur, Ga 30034

SKIDMORE, Catherine O.
c/o W. E. Ornstead
24802 Marine View Dr.
Zenith, Wash.

SMITH, Kathleen D.
c/o D. B. Smith
3709 29th St.
Bremerton, Wash

SMITH, Kathleen N.
c/o G. Smith
7929 W. 80th St.
Playa Del Rey, Ca 90291

SMITH, Patricia R.
c/o D. Varney
P.O. Box 226
Honaunau, Hawaii 96726

SPRING, William B.
c/o W. B. Spring
1006 East Lawn Ave.
Urbana, Ohio

STEELE, Nancy E.
c/o O. Steele
705 W. Park
Butte, Mont. 59701

SWEENEY, Patricia A.
c/o R. H. Sweeney
2953 Seminary Dr.
Greensburg, Pa 15601

THOMAS, Ernestine
c/o T. Jones
11205 Monticello Ave.
Silver Springs, Md.

TRAYLOR, Janet L.
c/o M. L. Traylor
116 Schilling
Moses Lake, Va

ULRICH, Teresa Ann
LTC (Ret) C. D. Ulrich
2238 Stratford Lane
Colorado, Springs, Colo 80909

WARD, Jeannette M.
c/o O. K. Ward
1325 W. Ironwood
Phoenix, Ariz. 85021

WINK, Paula J.
c/o H. P. Wink
5048 Trimble Rd.
Toledo, Ohio 43613

WOLFE, Roberta E.
c/o J. C. Wolfe
614 Opal St.
Huntington, Ind

WOOD, Susan B.
c/o R. P. Benson
11310 Stephan La.
Beltsville, Md 20705

WOODRUFF, Bridget
c/o J. Woodruff
90 Burlingame
Detroit, Mich 48202

WOXLAND, Christy M.
c/o S. A. Woxland
Rushford, Minn.

YANK, Christine L.
c/o F. A. Yank
672 N. 74th St.
Wauwatosa, Wis 53213

YEAGER, Kay H.
c/o H. J. Yeager
Rt. 7, Box 112
Ft. Collins, Colo 80521

YOUNG, Susan A.
c/o J. P. Adkins
805 Park St., Box 246
Mountain View, Okla

ZURAWSKI, Barbara A.
CPT E. Zurawski
319 Hayes Cr.
Ft. Ord, Calif.

A little warmth goes a long way . . .

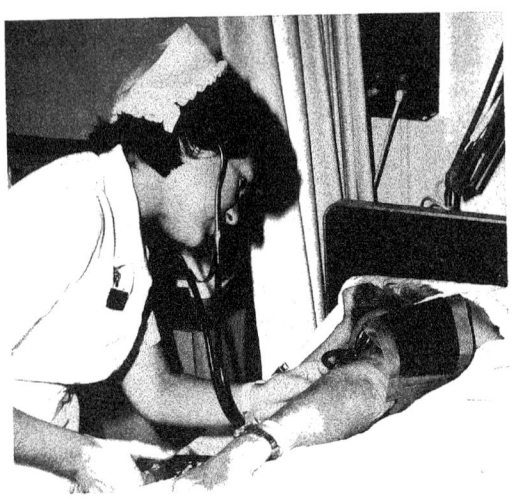
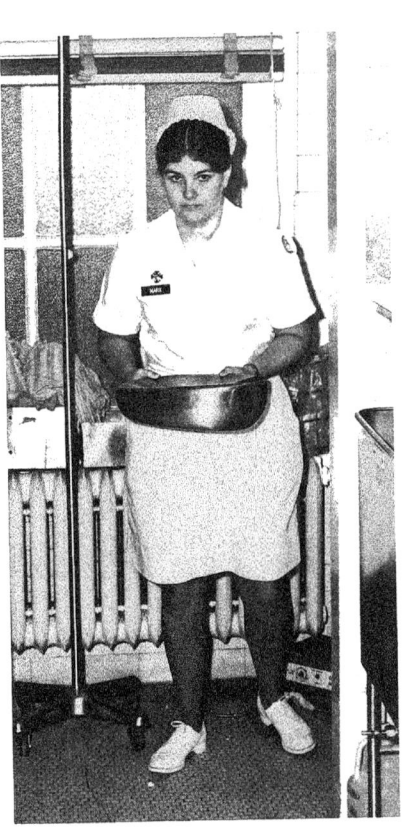

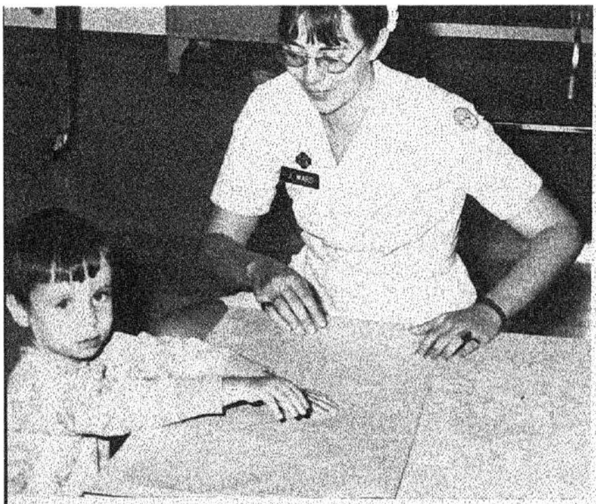

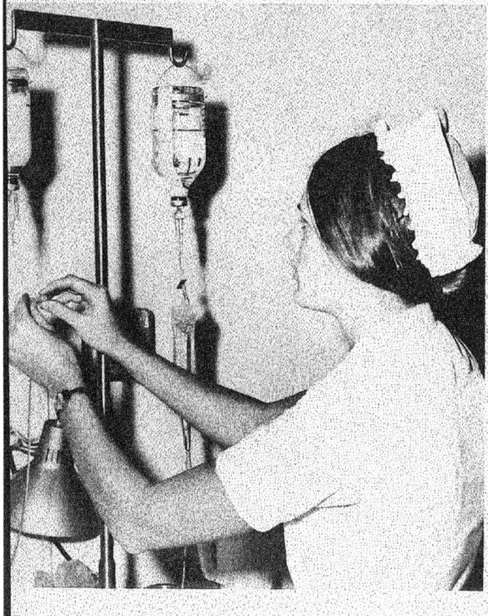

Collecting
Data
Through
Various
Routes??

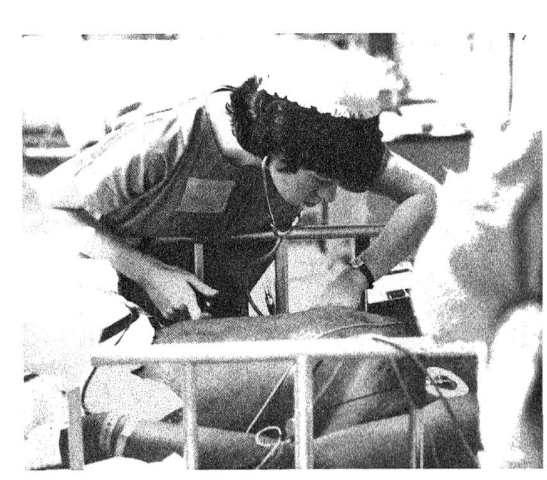

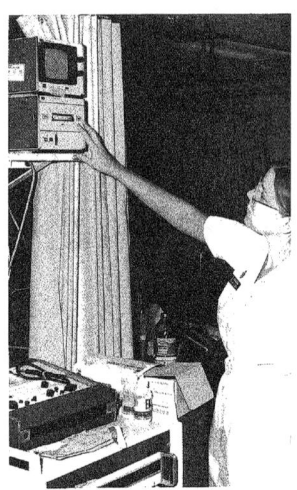

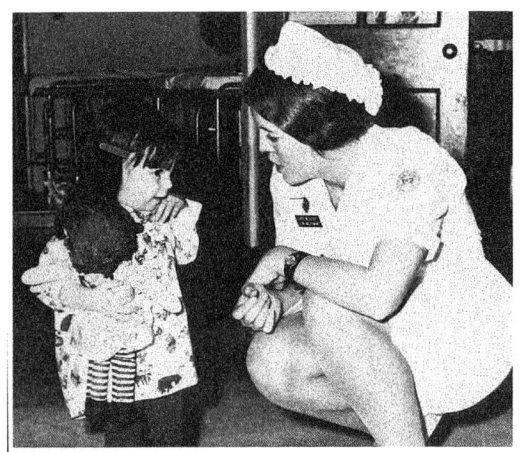
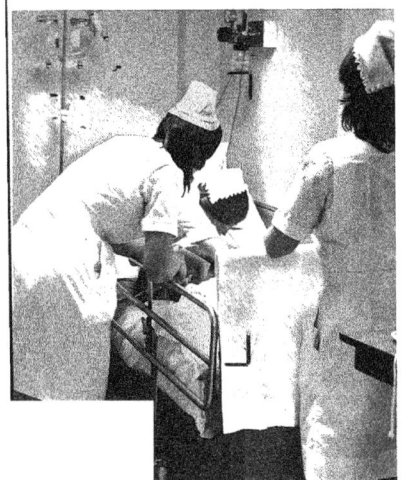

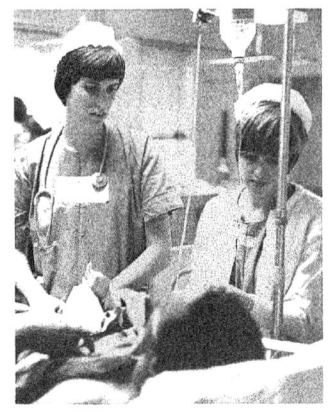
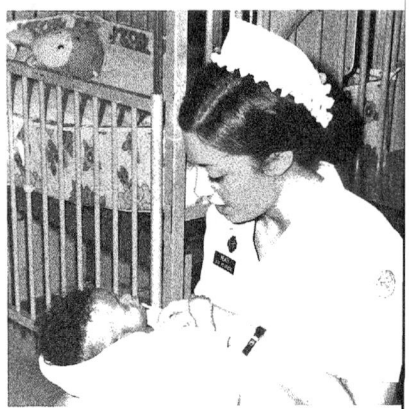

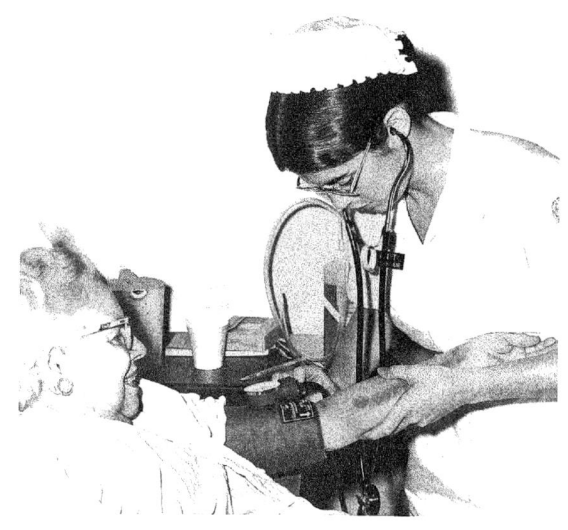
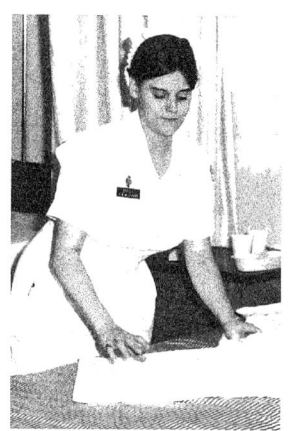
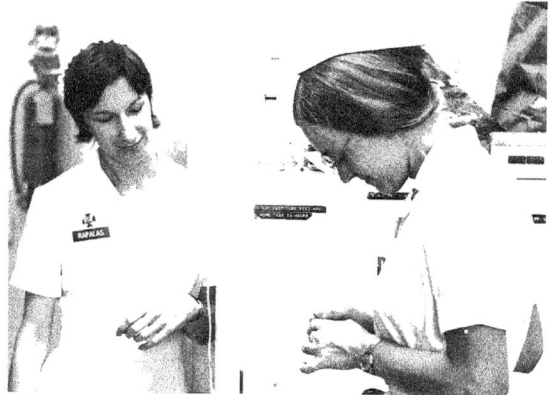

We've only just begun!
Everytime I evaluate
I find I'm never done · · ·

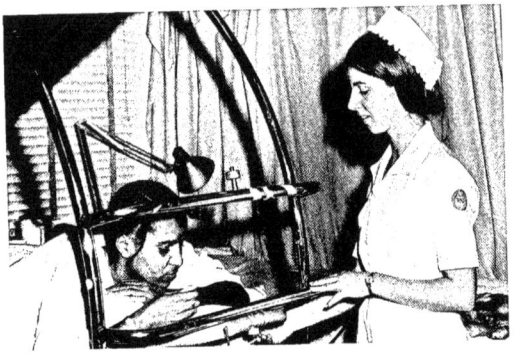

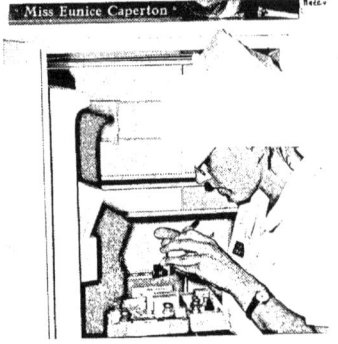

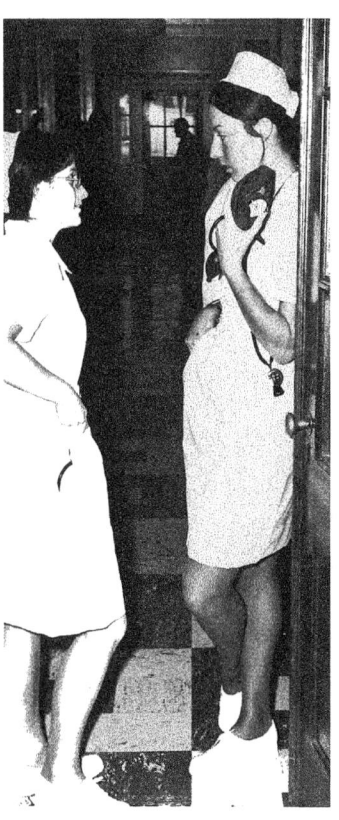
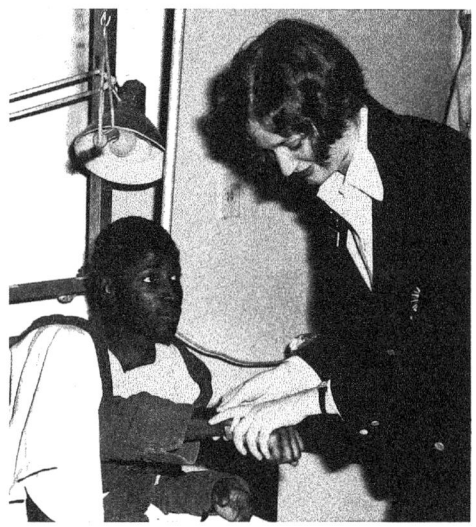

Learning new roles
In a variety of settings
Juniors always ask,
"Are you sure that's what we should be getting?"

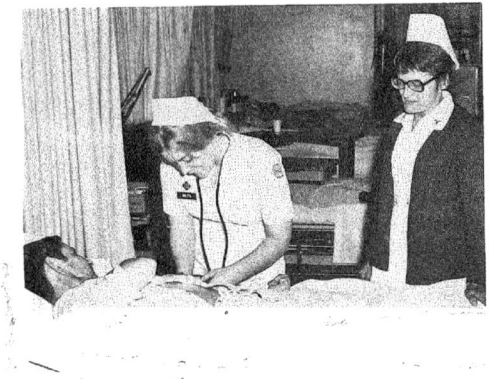
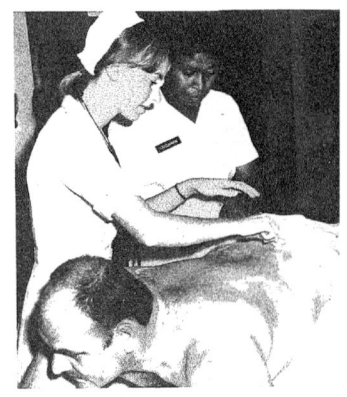

We
Finally
Made
It!

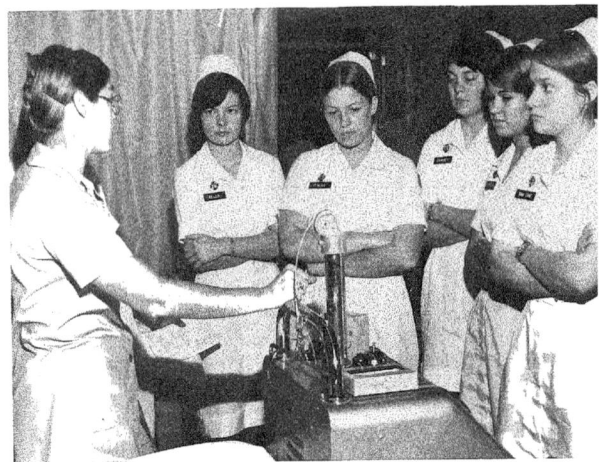

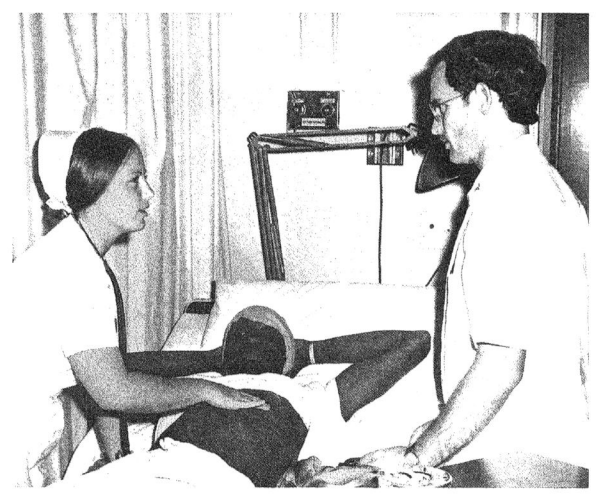

Let's
 Play
  Nurse
   Today.

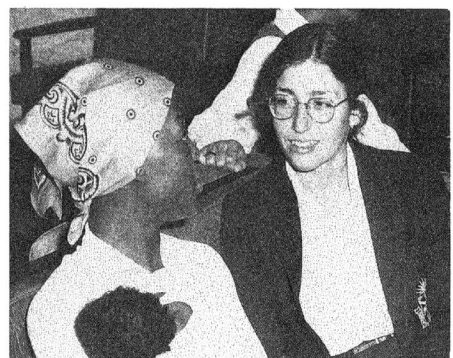
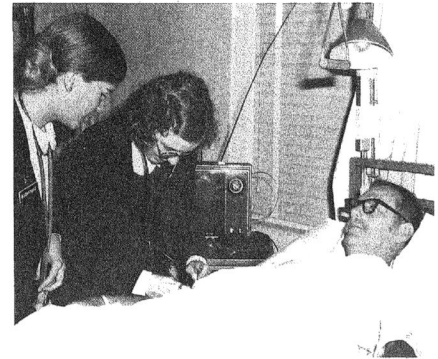

Planning for Tomorrow
Means talking things over today.
Congratulations, Juniors,
You're on your way.

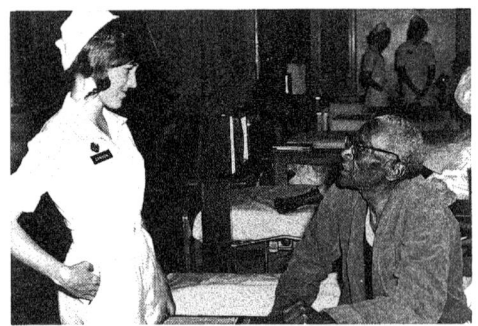

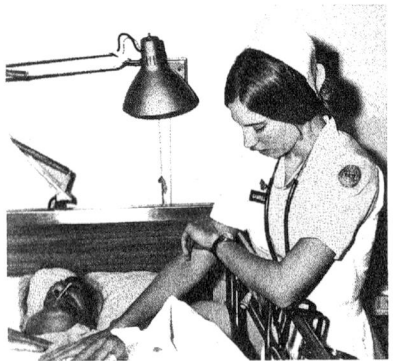

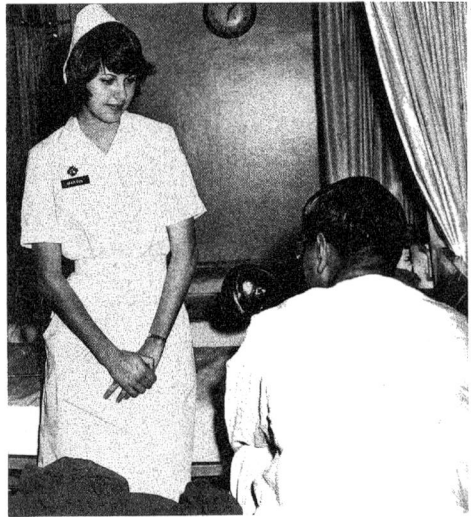

AND THIS IS ONLY THE FIRST WEEK

Standing in lines
Signing papers
Hurry up and wait
Shots, Greetings, Rules
Mess hall stares
Tours, Assignments.

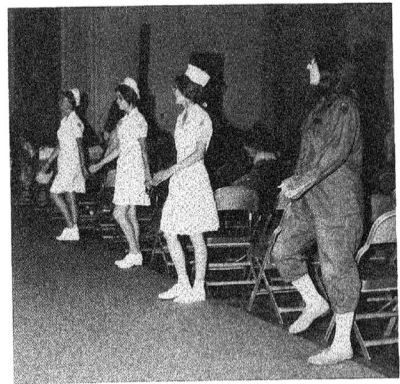

You're in the Army now.

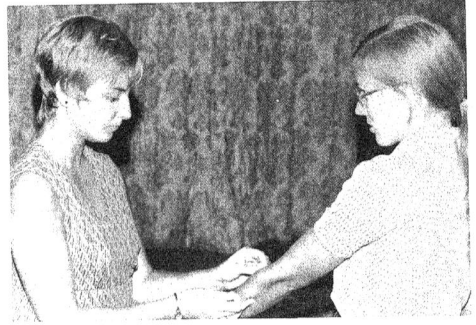

Are you sure you know what you're doing?

Welcome to WRAIN

All right women — shape up

Did you hear that?!

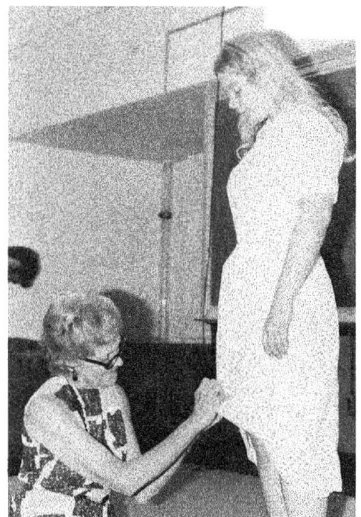
Below the knee — are you kidding?

This sure beats the mess hall.

Where do we go now?

Are you a male nurse?

Are these sack lunches?

Who said registration was

So these are the future Army Nurses!

Did you

STUDENT NURSES' ASSOCIATION OF MARYLAND

Practice makes perfect: Janice Piccioli, Transportation chmn.; Geri McCarty, President; Belle Rowan, Secretary; Keri Klotzbuecher, Nominations Committee Chmn.; Becky Burchfield, Treasurer; "client" Robin Bechtel, Historian. Not pictured: Gretchen Dickrell, Vice Pres.; Anne Leisering Project Committee Chmn.

The Student Nurses' Association of Maryland functions to introduce students to the responsibilities of nurses as professionals, within the community. Emphasis is placed on legislation concerning health care, nurse practice legislation and current issues related to health care. By creating an awareness of these issues early, SNAM members hope to enhance their participation in the delivery of health care, and the profession of nursing.

"How should I know?"
MAJ Lila Stevens, Advisor

Palm Reading; part of total nursing care?

I thought the pyramids were in Egypt.

What are you waiting for, the Great Pumpkin?

WRAIN CHOIR

Winter Christmas Concert

Major Washington gives a little advice.

A little louder girls.

"Carol of the Mistletoe Singers"

"I Wonder as I Wander"

"My Favorite Things"

Many enjoy — "An Old-Fashioned Christmas"

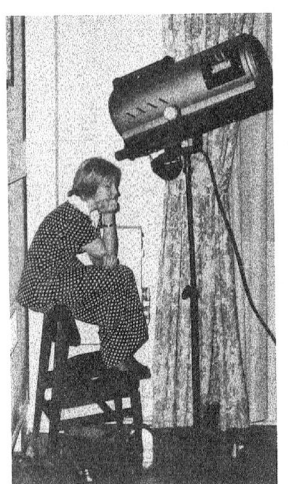
Behind the scenes

"Christ Child, Christ Child"

Are we ready to sing?

DISTRICT OF COLUMBIA STUDENT NURSES' ASSOCIATION

D.C.S.N.A. is the district's division of the National Student Nurse's Association, made up of students enrolled in schools of nursing within the boundaries of the District of Columbia. DCSNA attempts to promote active involvement with the concerns facing the nursing profession today. It addresses itself through discussion and activity to such issues as the changing role of nursing in the health care system, the nurse as collaborator with other health professionals, and the development of nursing awareness of community needs. Such attention is directed toward the personal and professional growth of the student with an increasing awareness and acceptance of her responsibility to herself, her profession, and her society.

STUDENT GOVERNMENT ORGANIZATION

L.-R. Carolyn Sanger, Social Chairman; Patricia Root, Senior Senator; Mary Ann Auerill, Secretary; Jesse Lobb, Yearbook Editor; Bill Spring, President; Sarah Fearn, Senior Class President; Susan Young, Chorus Co-Chairman; Kathy France, Treasurer; Marylou Robinson, Vice-President. Not pictured: Jim Parham, Jr. Class President.

SUBSYSTEM FUNCTIONING

Affiliative — A letter from home

Eliminative — Another day has passed!

Nutritive input at the good ole Mess Hall

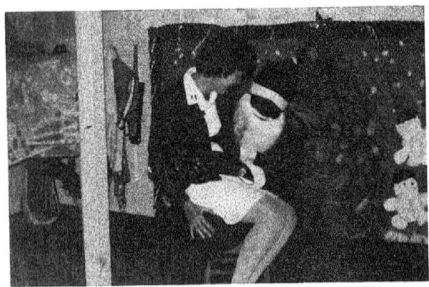

Affiliative — Santa Jim and the kiddies.

Restorative — Those early morning classes

Nutritive — Eating with the ants

Actuative — Counting Calories

Who am I?
What am I?

Affiliative — And you guys work with all these women?

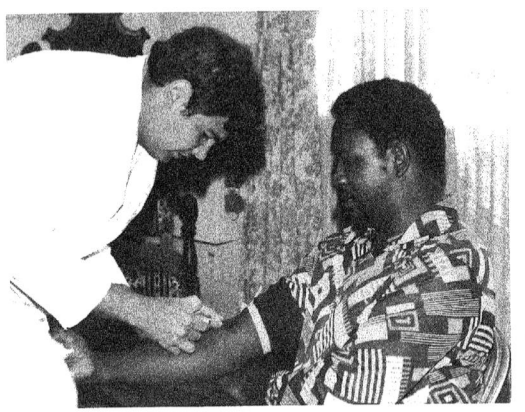

Protective — A volunteer donation?

Reproductive Information

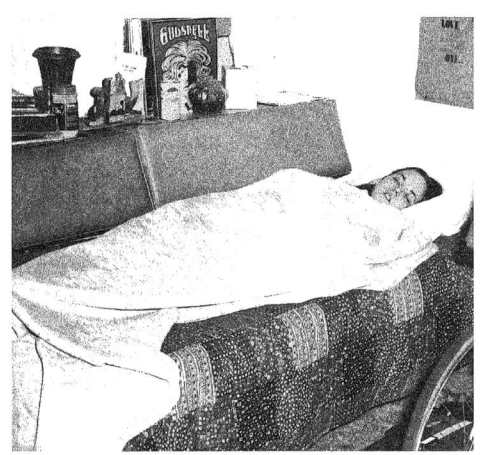
Restorative — Getting ready for another rough day.

The results of the Reproductive Subsystem at work.

Affiliative — Trick-or-Treat

Actuative — If I'm OK, then you're OK.

CHRISTMAS TIME

Food
Music
Finals
Children
Friends

GOING HOME!

AT DELANO HALL

THE LIFE OF A WRAIN

A little group therapy

Beautiful dames at the 50's Dance

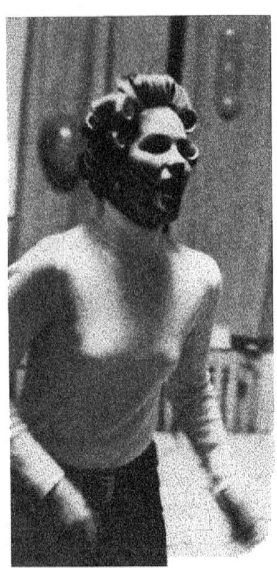

Stress!!

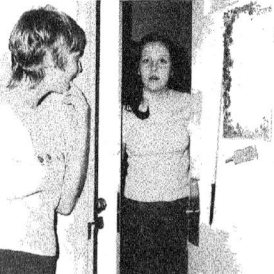

Who's there?

"Hello, mother?"

Sticking up for the Army

Another term paper — due tomorrow

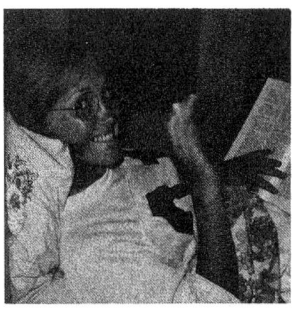

Studying?

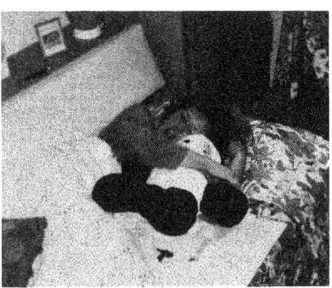

Companionship

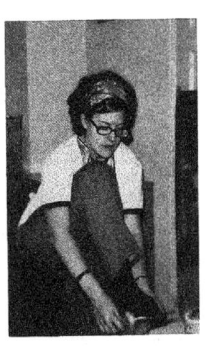

Getting the job done.

"If everyone lit just one little candle, what a bright worl

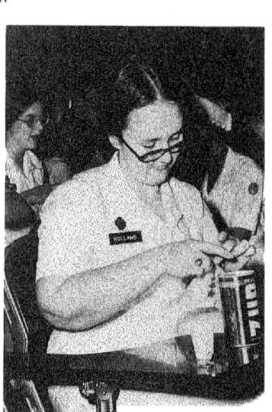

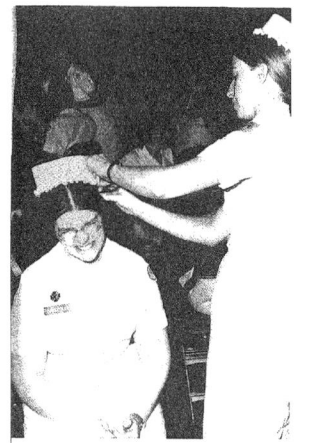
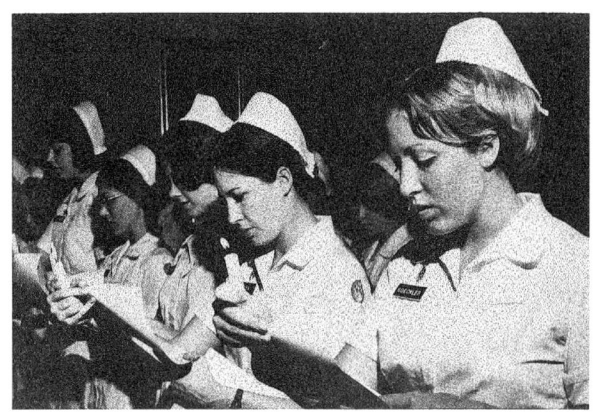

"As a nurse, I pledge..."

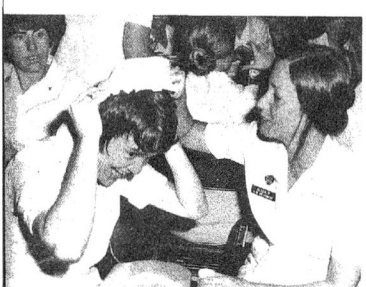
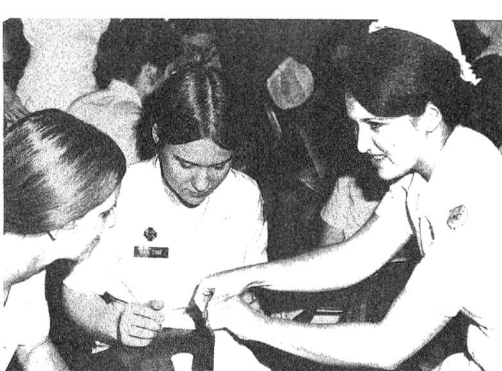

"Now, this is how it's done."

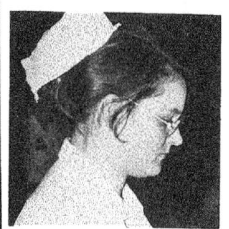

"BECAUSE I'M A NURSE"

JUNIOR CLASS FORMAL
February 23, 1974

PATRONS

MAJ Clara L. Adams
Mr. & Mrs. Monico Almachar
MAJ Betty J. Antille
1LT Rebecca Azares
Mr. & Mrs. Furman S. Baldwin
1LT & Mrs. Robert E. Barnwell
Mr. & Mrs. Kenneth Behlen
Mr. & Mrs. Robert P. Benson
Mrs. Ann Berg
Mr. & Mrs. Owen A. Berg
1LT Susan M. Birkel
COL & Mrs. Dean G. Boyle
MAJ Betty Brice
Mr. & Mrs. Raymond Brosius
Dr. & Mrs. George C. Brown
Mr. & Mrs. Marion R. Bryson
Mr. & Mrs. Samuel Burchfield
Mr. & Mrs. David Burkhardt
Mrs. Florence E. Burns
Mr. & Mrs. Roy N. Carlson
1LT Cathleen Carnahan
Mr. & Mrs. John P. Combs
Dr. & Mrs. Edward W. Deska
MAJ Kathleen Devin
Mr. & Mrs. Don L. Dover
LTC & Mrs. S. A. Fede
Mr. & Mrs. Charles E. George

1LT Jan L. Keller
Mr. & Mrs. Albert E. Kirk
Mr. & Mrs. E. E. Klotzbuecher
1LT Connie Knudson
LTC & Mrs. C. M. Landis
Mr. & Mrs. Howard J. Lobb
CPT & Mrs. Joseph P. Maloney
Mr. & Mrs. Frank McCarty
Mrs. Adelaide D. McGovern
CPT Elizabeth McGowan
Mrs. Mary C. Meighen
Mr. & Mrs. J. D. Mottley, Jr.
Mr. & Mrs. Edward C. Muse
Mr. & Mrs. Andre T. Norman
Mr. & Mrs. Walter O'Connor
Mrs. Ida R. Osman
CPT Linda L. Pape
Mr. & Mrs. Norman Pepin
Arthur Piccioli
LTC & Mrs. George Poppas, Jr.
Mrs. Mary E. Railey
CPT Janet Rexrod
Mr. & Mrs. Walter J. Robinson
Mr. & Mrs. James W. Root
LTC Miriam G. Rotschild
Mr. & Mrs. John B. Shrewsbury
LTC Norma R. Small

SPONSORS

Mr. & Mrs. Adam C. Ade
Mr. & Mrs. George B. Akers
Mr. & Mrs. Robert S. Averell
Mr. & Mrs. Robert Baehr
COL. & Mrs. C. F. Baish, Jr.
Mr. & Mrs. Frank J. Bala
LTC Marian C. Barbieri
COL. & Mrs. Wm. E. Bartholdt
Mr. & Mrs. Wm. H. Bernard
LTC Ellen M. Berg
Mr. & Mrs. Raymond Blaase
Mrs. Herta M. Clark
Mr. & Mrs. Alfred L. Conte
Mr. & Mrs. L. A. Dallenbach
COL. & Mrs. Clifford Dorsey
MAJ F. E. Ferington
Mr. & Mrs. Wm. S. Flanagan
Mr. & Mrs. William Fletcher
Mr. & Mrs. Charles R. France
Mr. & Mrs. Bernhart G. Fred
CPT & Mrs. Gunnar Frederiksen
Dr. & Mrs. John E. Goeckler
LTC. & Mrs. George S. Goodale
Mr. & Mrs. Ray Halopka
LTC & Mrs. Charles V. Heath
Mr. & Mrs. Martin W. Hesselman
LTC Ann Hiers
Mr. & Mrs. George W. Hill, Jr.
Robert H. Hoisington
1LT Carol Holland
Dr. & Mrs. Lloyd Halbert
Mr. & Mrs. Lewis Humke
Mr. & Mrs. Bruce Jerney
MAJ Joyce G. Johnson
LTC & Mrs. John H. Karwoski
Rose Ann (Blahusch) Kassel
Mr. & Mrs. Richard D. Key
Mr. & Mrs. John F. Kinder

Mr. & Mrs. Harding Kindrick
Mr. & Mrs. Fred T. Kishaba
Mr. & Mrs. Drew Lansberry
CPT & Mrs. Paul C. Learmann
1LT Jean A. Linton
LTC Betty Jane Lynch
Mr. & Mrs. Leo G. Marx
Mr. & Mrs. Wallace McNeil
Mr. & Mrs. Geo. R. Mettey
COL. & Mrs. Wm. R. Miller
LTC. Hannah S. Moynahan
Mrs. Elaine Munoz
Mr. & Mrs. Wm. J. Murison
Marion I. Murphy
Mr. & Mrs. S. J. Nakanishi
Mr. & Mrs. William J. Norton III
LTC Joyce J. Nurse
Mr. & Mrs. John O'Leary
Mr. & Mrs. Willis R. Penn
COL. Drusilla Poole
Mr. & Mrs. Clemens O. Putz
Mr. & Mrs. John J. Rendos
1LT Robyn Richardson
Mr. & Mrs. Frank Rincon
1LT Carol S. Russell
Mr. & Mrs. Michelle A. Schmidt
CPT Rosamond Shepard
CWO & Mrs. John E. Snyder, Sr.
MAJ Lila C. Stevens
1LT Barbara Tallman
Mr. & Mrs. M. L. Traylor
LTC. & Mrs. Alfred N. Tucker
Mr. & Mrs. Bobby J. Vandergriff
Mr. & Mrs. Neil Van Tine
COL. & Mrs. George A. Westphal
Mr. & Mrs. Frank Yank
Mr. & Mrs. Edward Zurawski

CPSIA information can be obtained
at www.ICGtesting.com
Printed in the USA
BVHW040929101218
535233BV00020B/1020/P